Pinocchio

CHAPTER 2

Illustrated by Suzane Langlois

A woodcutter was walking through a forest.
There he found an amazing piece of wood.
The wood laughed and cried just like a boy.

The woodcutter took the wood to his friend Geppetto because Geppetto was a puppetmaker.

As soon as Geppetto carved the puppet's feet, the puppet jumped up.

"My name is Pinocchio," the puppet said.

Then Pinocchio ran right out the door.

Poor Geppetto!
He already loved Pinocchio like a son.
But Pinocchio was a puppet.
He did not know how to love.

Soon Pinocchio was lost and hungry.
A good fairy found him.
She took him home and gave him dinner.

Pinocchio told the fairy that he wished to be a real boy.

"You must learn how to be good," said the fairy. "When you learn that, you will become a real boy."

Pinocchio did not learn to be good right away.
He told a lie to the fairy.
And every time Pinocchio told a lie, his nose grew.

Pinocchio told a lie in the morning.
He told a lie at night.
His nose grew and grew!
Pinocchio was ashamed.
He ran away from the fairy's house.

All this time, Geppetto searched for Pinocchio. He searched high and low.

He even searched the ocean.
His boat was caught in a storm.

Meanwhile, Pinocchio kept getting into trouble. Someone even threw him into the sea.

Pinocchio tried to swim back to shore, but a giant whale swallowed him.

Can you guess who Pinocchio met in the whale's belly?
It was Geppetto!
The whale had swallowed him, too.

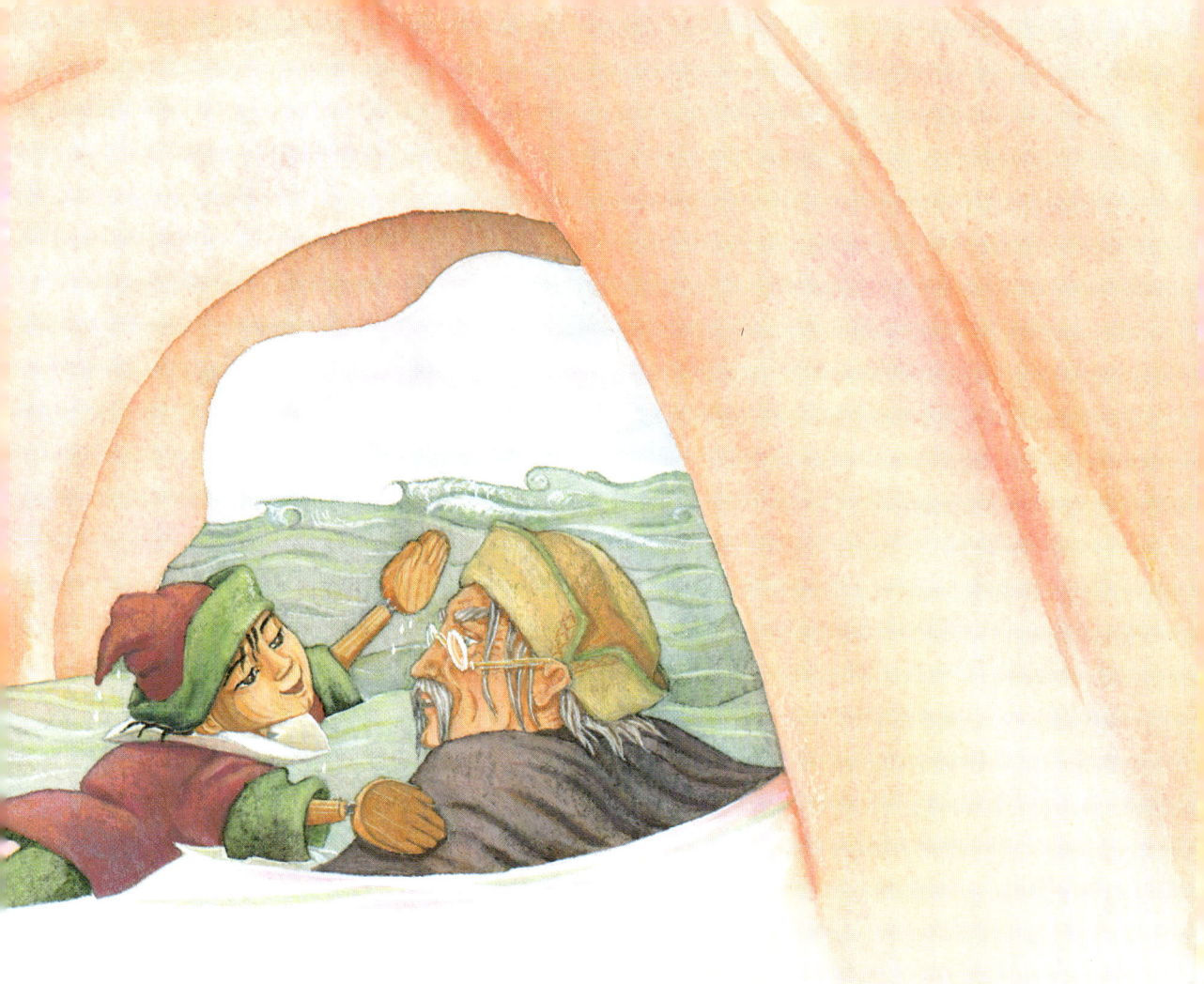

Pinocchio and Geppetto were able to escape through the whale's mouth. But they weren't out of danger yet.

"Help me. I can't swim!" Geppetto cried.

Pinocchio helped Geppetto swim to shore.

"Thank you, Pinocchio. You are a good boy," Geppetto said.

Pinocchio hugged and kissed Geppetto.
Pinocchio's wish had come true.
He was a real boy at last!